Go Daddy Go!

Written by
STEVINA EVULEOCHA

Illustrations by
HABIBAH UGBAH

Dedication & Acknowledgements

Dedicated to my dad whose political journey taught me the sacrifices of a political family, to the people of Benue who supported the Ishor Chenji movement, and to the memory of Johnny.

Special thanks to Nene Kumashe Ugbah for her tireless help and support in preparing this story, and my god-daughter Naomi Ike who read the story and gave us her perspective.

My name is Kachi! I was born in Walnut Creek, California. I am the fourth of five kids in my family. My parents are Nigerian-Americans who originally came to the U.S. to go to school. They met while in college and decided to stay in the U.S. and start a family. My mom is Ibo-speaking from Southeastern Nigeria. My dad is Tiv-speaking from North Central Nigeria, also known as the Middle Belt. I visited Nigeria for the first time when I was five years old.

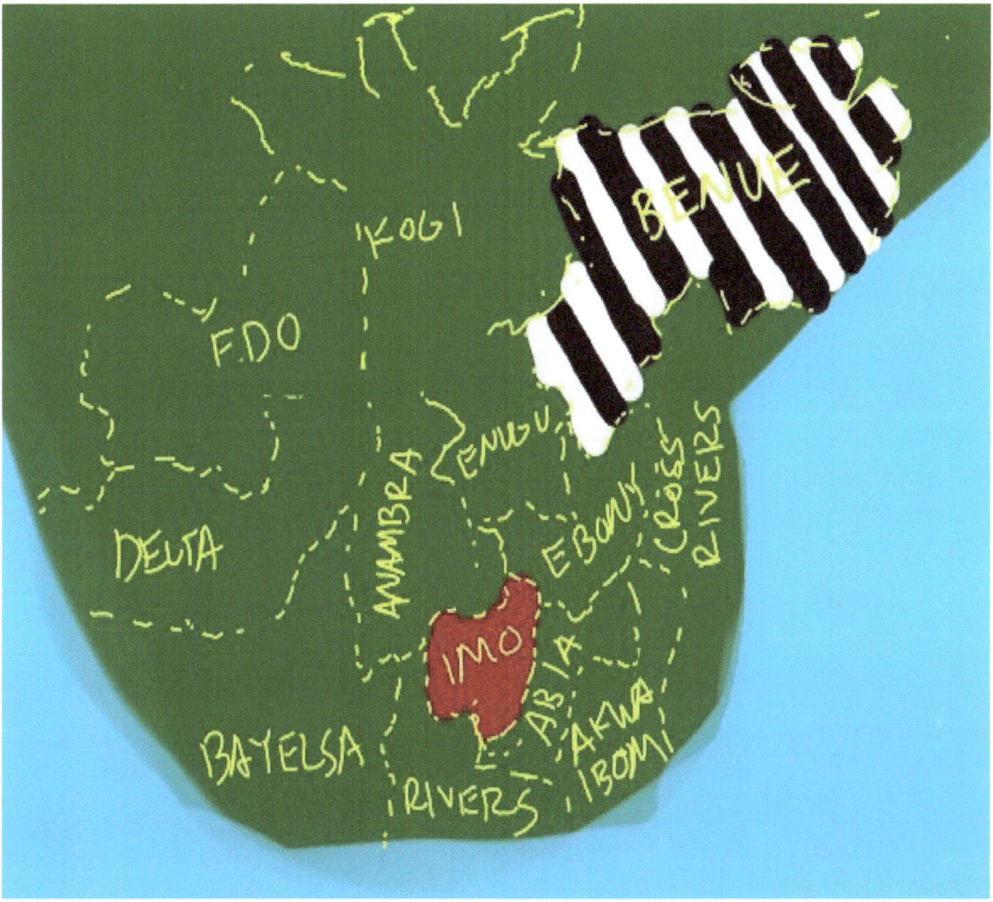

KOGI
BENUE
EDO
ENUGU
ANAMBRA
DELTA
EBONYI
CROSS RIVERS
IMO
ABIA
AKWA IBOM
BAYELSA
RIVERS

During our trip, I met so many uncles, aunties, and cousins, and my grandparents! My Grandpa Paul, on my dad's side, always sipped delicious lemon tea with me whenever I visited him. My Grandpa Steve, on my mom's side, always cooked amazing meals for my siblings and I whenever we visited him. My dad's mother, Grandma Cecilia, died before I was born, so I never met her. But I got to spend a week in Owerri with my mom's mother, Grandma Bridget, during my family's visit to Nigeria!

Long before our trip to Nigeria, Mom always reminded us that we were Nigerian-Americans, and that we should be proud of both cultures. To make sure we didn't forget our Tiv culture, Mom planned our annual family vacations to different states around the U.S. where summer Tiv meetings were held. It was always fun getting to know other Tiv kids who had similar stories to tell about their lives.

MDZOUGH U TIV
AYATUTU KAUNO? KA SE

One year, when our parents couldn't afford to fly us to the meeting, our family decided to drive three days one-way to attend the Tiv meeting in Atlanta. On the way to Atlanta, we stopped along the way and visited even more uncles, aunties, and cousins who lived in some of the states on our route to Atlanta. I still remember that it took us forever to cross Texas!

After we came back from Atlanta, I started fourth grade. That Thanksgiving, Mom said we were going to my auntie's house to celebrate.

"Yipee!", I thought, "Time to hang out with my cousins! I must remember to bring things we can do because we usually leave from auntie's house late at night."

Mom and Dad were acting rather funny that night. They called my three older sisters to a meeting in their room. Mom and Dad told my baby brother and I to go to sleep. My brother and I went to bed wondering why we were not included in the family meeting.

On Thanksgiving Day, we set out for the one and half hour drive to my auntie's house. I couldn't wait to see my cousins! This Thanksgiving, all my cousins, aunties, and uncles from my dad's side of the family were present. I couldn't be happier!

My dad cooked the turkey for Thanksgiving as he normally does, and we brought it to auntie's house. My auntie made a lot of yummy dishes. Everyone ate Thanksgiving dinner together. After dinner was over, my cousins and I played, we ate, we watched movies, and we ate some more!

When it was dark outside, my big sister told us younger ones to go upstairs because the adults were having a meeting downstairs and didn't want to be disturbed. My big sister told us we could go to the kitchen to get food or drink, but we were to leave quietly right after.

Every time I went to the kitchen to get some snacks, my parents, uncles, and aunties were huddled together. They looked very serious and talked in low tones. No one was smiling. I wondered what they were talking about. But I was having so much fun with my cousins that I didn't let it bother me! My baby brother and I must have fallen asleep before we left auntie's house. We woke up the next day in our house.

A few days after Thanksgiving, Mom told my brother and I that Dad would be travelling to Nigeria to do some work and wouldn't be home for Christmas. Before this time, we had never spent Christmas with anyone in my family absent. This was new! Why was Dad going to Nigeria? Why did he need another job? Both of my parents were college professors. I asked so many questions, but Mom said not to worry, Dad will be back soon! I already missed Dad.

I started to miss Dad even before he left. On the day Dad left, we all went to the airport to see him off. I knew it was serious when I saw my oldest sister crying. I had never seen her cry. Mom had a poker face the whole time and tried to cheer everyone up. Soon, Dad walked past security at the airport, and we stood and watched him take a few steps and wave, and we'd wave back. We continued to wave to him until he crossed security and flashed one more smile at us before walking away from view to board his waiting plane.

The drive home was quiet and somber. My big sister suggested we get some donuts. Mom agreed, almost relieved that we wanted to do something outside the house. When we got home from buying donuts, we all sat around our kitchen table and ate in silence. Everyone needed the sugar for comfort. Mom joined us to eat donuts, which were not her thing. No one talked about Dad, but he was on everyone's mind.

That night, we went to bed without saying our bedtime prayers.

Christmas was hard without Dad. We told Mom we wanted to spend Christmas at home in honor of Dad, and that family members could spend Christmas at home with us. Luckily, our uncles and aunties understood, and all came over. Dad bought the tallest Christmas tree we ever had before going to Nigeria. We had a full house for Christmas, and the best part of Christmas was the Wii game system that Mom gave us as a gift! We all enjoyed playing the many games on the Wii until the end of winter break.

Winter was slow. Mom made sure we spoke to Dad often. It didn't make missing him easy, and I still had questions. I would ask him every time we spoke on the phone when he was coming back to California, and he would say "soon." One day, Dad told us he would send some videos to us so we could see what he was doing in Nigeria. We were so excited; we even went to pick the videos up with Mom. When we got back and tried to play the videos, the format didn't allow us to play any of them. The next day, Mom took the videos to a photo place and asked them to convert the disk to a format we could watch.

One of my older sisters was home from college the weekend Mom got the videos back. We went up to our parents' room and all sat around to watch the video. What we saw was interesting and puzzling at the same time. Dad was in all the videos and was always surrounded by a lot of people. Everywhere he went, they all seemed happy to see him and sang songs with his name. Everyone around him held a broom in their hand. When I asked Mom about it, she said the broom was the symbol of Dad's political party.

When the video finished, Mom was on the hot seat. My big sisters understood what was happening in the videos, but my brother and I had many questions, and wanted to know why Dad was always surrounded by large crowds of people. Mom told us Dad was running for governor of Benue State in Nigeria, and the people in the videos were his supporters.

When we asked when the elections will be held, Mom said April of the following year. "Dad's going to be gone for four months?" I asked. My big sister said he was doing it to help people in Nigeria, and that we should be happy for him and the people of Benue, our home state. It was hard to be happy for people I didn't know, who spent more time with Dad than we did.

What did this mean? Was Dad never coming back to California? What about my soccer games? My trips with Dad to Barnes & Noble to read books and get ice cream on the way home? If Dad wins, would we have to leave our lives in California and move to Nigeria? Would we be able to make new friends? Would we ever come back to our house in California? Too many questions on my mind! Mom said we'd make decisions about what to do as a family when Dad wins the election.

Although I didn't understand all the details, all I knew was that our family life was changing very fast, and I didn't know how to stop it. Already, Mom had asked the school district to allow me transfer to my brother's school which was a walking distance from my sister's high school, to reduce the number of pick-ups Mom would do. My sister waited with us afterschool until Mom rushed back between her classes to take us home and go back to teach her night class. Mom scheduled it such that my two older sisters who were in college took turns baby-sitting us on Skype while she went to her night class two days a week.

After we saw the videos, all I kept thinking was how it was like my Dad to help others every chance he got.

That night, as I lay next to my teddy bear that hugged like my Dad, all I kept chanting in my head was **"Go Daddy Go!"** until I drifted off to sleep and dreamt mostly about my Dad.

www.ingramcontent.com/pod-product-compliance
Lightning Source LLC
LaVergne TN
LVHW021350160826
845679LV00008B/1563

* 9 7 9 8 8 4 4 5 4 3 7 8 4 *